पति Pati
Husband
In the eyes of wife

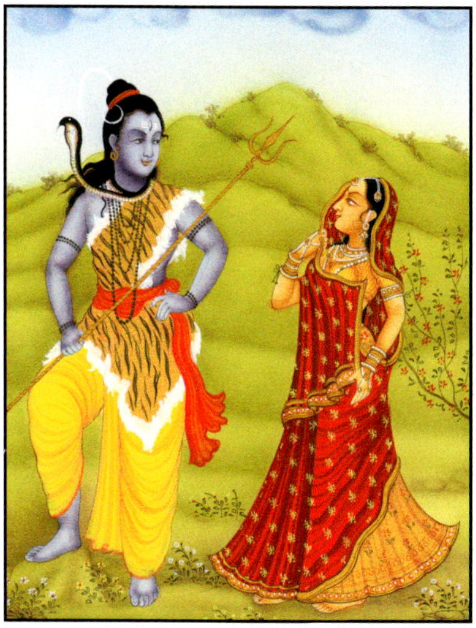

R.N. Kogata • Lalita Kogata

D.K. Printworld (P) Ltd.
New Delhi

Cataloging in Publication Data — DK
[Courtesy: D.K. Agencies (P) Ltd. <docinfo@dkagencies.com>]

Kogata, R. N. (Ram Narayan), 1964–
Pati = Husband : in the eyes of wife /
R.N. Kogata, Lalita Kogata.
p. cm.
English and Hindi.
ISBN 13: 9788124604830
ISBN 10: 8124604835

1. Husbands — Prayers and devotions. 2. Man-woman relationships in art. 3. Spouses in art. 4. Love in art. 5. Siva (Hindu deity) — Art. 6. Parvati (Hindu deity) — Art. 7. Art, Hindu. I. Kogata, Lalita, 1965–, joint author. II. Title. III. Title: Husband : in the eyes of wife.

DDC 306.872 22

First Published in India, 2009
ISBN 13: 978-81-246-0483-0
ISBN 10: 81-246-0483-5

A Creation of:
Mr. R.N. Kogata
Mrs. Lalita Kogata
608, Hiran Magari, Sector-11, Udaipur - India
Phone : +91-94141-58870
devkush@rediffmail.com

Published and printed by:
D.K. Printworld (P) Ltd.
'Sri Kunj' F-52, Bali Nagar
Ramesh Nagar Metro Stn., New Delhi - 110015
Phs.: 011-2545 3975, 2546 6019
Fax: 011-2546 5926
Email: dkprintworld@vsnl.net
Web: www.dkprintworld.com

Pati पति Husband
In the eyes of wife

मितं ददाति हि पिता मितं भ्राता मितं सुतः।
अमितस्य प्रदातारं भर्तारं का न पूजयेत्॥

— मत्स्यपुराण, 210.18

पिता, भाई और पुत्र सीमित मात्रा में ही (सुख) देते हैं। असीम मात्रा में (सुख) देने वाले पति की कौन स्त्री पूजा नहीं करेगी?

Father, brother and sons only give limited (happiness to a woman). Which woman would then not adore a husband who gives unlimited (happiness)?

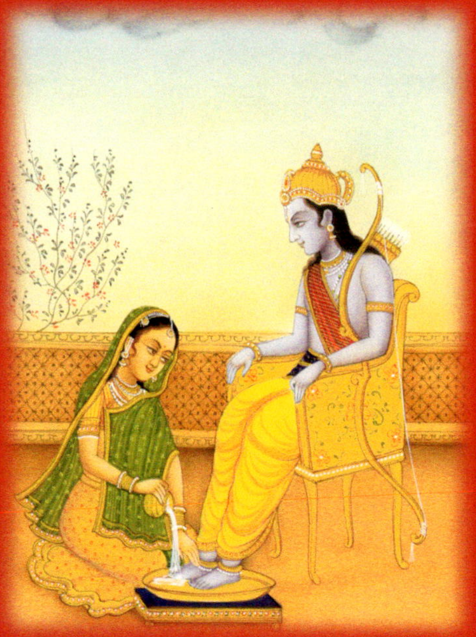

॥ ॐ गं गणपतये नमः ॥

Preface

It is said that it is far better to marry an old man or a poor or even an ugly man if he loves you, rather than to marry a young, rich and handsome bachelor who pays no heed to you.

A man is the leading householder and has many roles to play — a father, a son, a husband, a brother and so on — and he takes care of the whole family in all these roles. He earns the livelihood, sustain the family and society, perform some daily rites and repay the debts both financial and social. A man is always tested in four ways: with reference to his family, conduct, quality and action, just as gold is tested in four ways: by rubbing, breaking, heating and beating.

It is said that truth is male, faith is female; mind is husband, speech is wife; wherever the husband is, there is wife too. As husband, he is the pride and honour for wife; his role as friend and companion makes life smoother. A husband is source of dream and destination, he sets the way and speed, his positive attitude results in creativity, inspiration and happiness in the family, his love and affection creates a better environment in the family, and for a wife, the husband is the ultimate truth and shrine. Therefore, a husband should become part of her dreams and her friend; avoid inhibitions coming in the way; talk, walk and think together; understand and listen patiently; realize her hard work and sacrifice; encourage, respect and allow her to fulfil her wishes; pay her compliments and appreciate her work, gestures and ideas and do everything for her with inner joy of giving.

In our words, a caring husband has these ingredients - **H** for **H**umorous, **U** for **U**nderstanding, **S** for **S**trong, **B** for **B**old, **A** for **A**dventurous, **N** for **N**avigator and **D** for **D**emanding.

This book is a small attempt by us to express the love, affection, respect and feelings of a wife for her husband with the help of beautiful adjectives with the objective to inspire all the husbands to become perfect caring husbands.

We are grateful to His Highness Shreeji Arvind Singh Mewar for his worthy guidance from time to time. We prostrate before our parents Shri Bhairav Lal Kogata and Smt Kanchan Devi Kogata and Prof K.M. Nuwal and Smt Kamla Devi Nuwal and all our family members for their beloved blessings, without which we would not have reached this stage.

R.N. Kogata
Lalita Kogata

Importance of Husband

While giving away Sita in marriage to Rama, King Janaka of Mithila says, within a popular verse, *saha dharma caree tava,* i.e. Sita will be a co-traveller with Rama in his path of *dharma*. It implies that Rama, or a husband for that matter, is on a path of *dharma,* or should be on a path of *dharma.*

According to Manu, just as it is the duty of a wife to obey her husband, it is the bounden duty of a husband to protect his wife.

Marriage has three main purposes according to ancient Indian thought: (1) the promotion of religion by the performance of household sacrifices; (2) progeny, whereby the father and his ancestors were assured of a happy after-life and the line was continued; and (3) *rati,* or sexual pleasure. At the time of marriage, the bride's father formally gives the bride to the groom, who promises that "he would not behave falsely to her (the bride) in respect of the three traditional aims of life — piety or *dharma,* wealth or *artha,* and pleasure or *kaama.*" Religious merit or *dharma* should be gained through following the sacred Law — involving numerous religious duties notably the performance of birth, marriage, funeral and other ceremonies and the regular performance of five great sacrifices (*pancha mahaa yajna*) — wealth should be gained by honest means, and *kaama* means pleasure of all kinds.

It is stated in literature that a husband should lovingly cherish his wife, feed and care for her well and provide her with jewellery and luxuries to the limits of his means. The wife should never be upbraided too severely, for the gods will not accept the sacrifice of the man who beats his wife.

In a household we can't say who is more important, a husband or a wife. Both are halves and both join to make a whole. Until recently it was established that a husband should earn wealth to run the household and the wife should look after the husband and the children and run the house within the husband's earnings. In India a man after marriage is called a *grihastha* or householder or husband. A true *grihastha* is one who marries a girl who is separated from him by five generations on the maternal side and seven generations on the paternal side.

A true *grihastha* should daily worship *deva*s, cows, brahmins, scholars, old men and preceptors.

According to Amsa 3, *Vishnu Purana,* he should worship *sandhya* (dawn and dusk) daily, and also fire. He should never steal, speak unpleasant words to anybody nor speak an untruth even if it is pleasant. He should not openly speak about the sins of others. He should not covet another man's wife.

While circumambulating the sacred fire during marriage the bridegroom addresses his bride thus:

> O bride ! I am like *Saamaveda* and you are like *Rigveda.* You, like the earth, will remain cool and forgiving always, and remain in social life, whereas I, like the sun, will work hard continuously and regularly.

The circumambulation comprises seven rounds. The bride leads the first three rounds. The fourth round is performed by both the bridegroom and bride together. The fifth, sixth and seventh rounds are done by the bridegroom leading. The bride is shown in a leading role because it is only the woman who controls the family and the household affairs by her experience. The works like service, trading and those done outside the house, are usually performed by the man only, and therefore, for the last three rounds the wife follows the husband.

After the circumambulations, the husband and wife perform the ceremony of *Saptapadi* or walking together the first time the seven steps and begin their new life. While the first six steps are taken (1) for the growth of food, (2) for physical and mental growth, (3) for growth of wealth, (4) for growth of happiness, (5) for the proper performance of all duties, and (6) for following the right method, manner and custom of living according to seasons, the last and seventh step is taken for the wife's obedience to her husband, politeness and friendly nature. Here, the husband also promises and agrees to be noble, kind, friendly towards his wife and to be her follower always in life.

Neither the husband nor the wife is superior or inferior to the other. Both have an equal role to play in running a family efficiently. By adjusting themselves to any changed circumstances, and by destroying ego from their minds, the husband and wife can take position on each side of a yoke and pull the cart of married life, loaded with childern, with ease on the path of *dharma,* overcoming all trials and tribulations, towards the goal of peace and happiness.

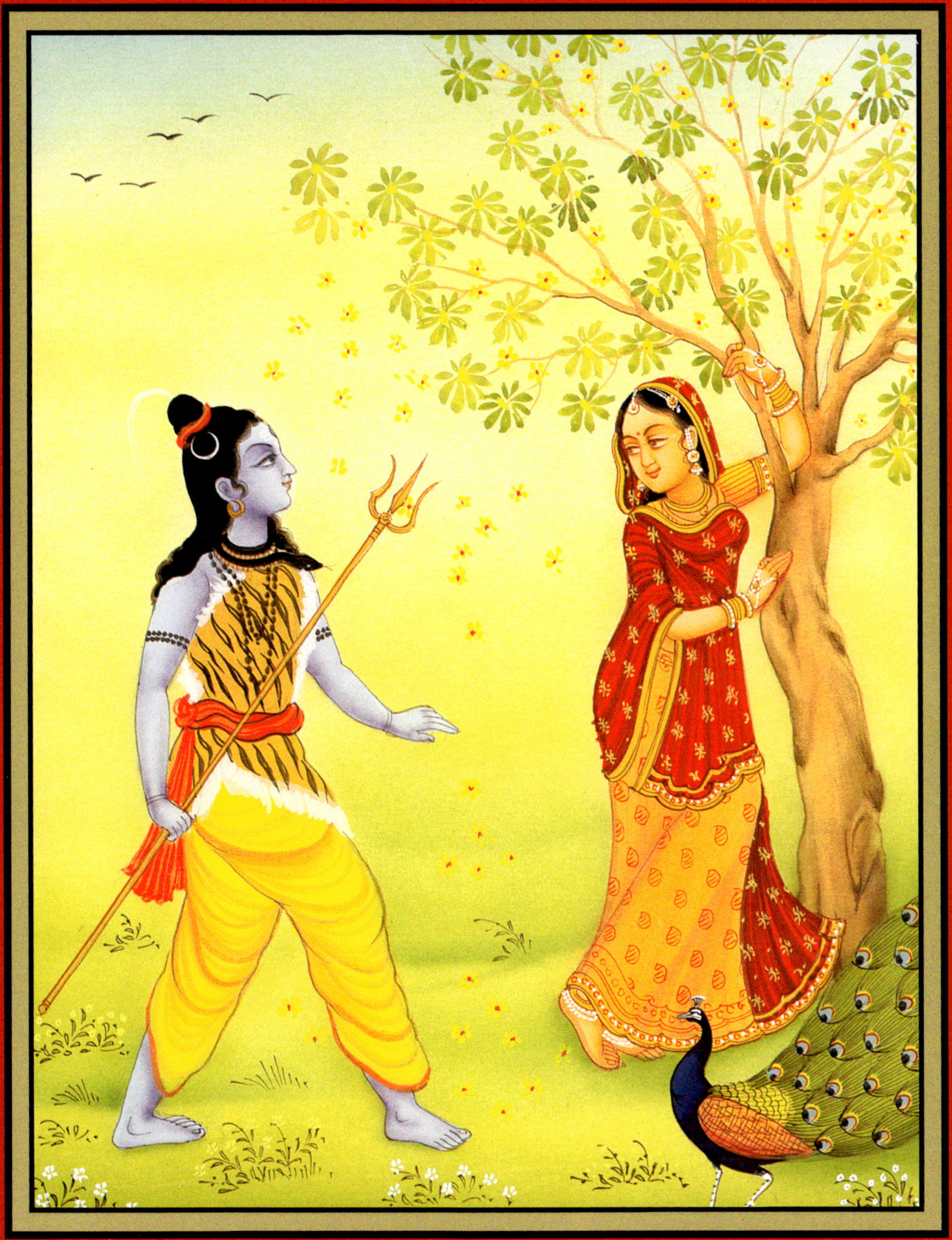

तू मेरा प्रेम है, इश्क है, प्यार है।
तुझसे ही मेरे जीवन में बहार है।।

Pati पति
Husband

You are my affection, my attachment, my love.
My life is full of bloom because of you.

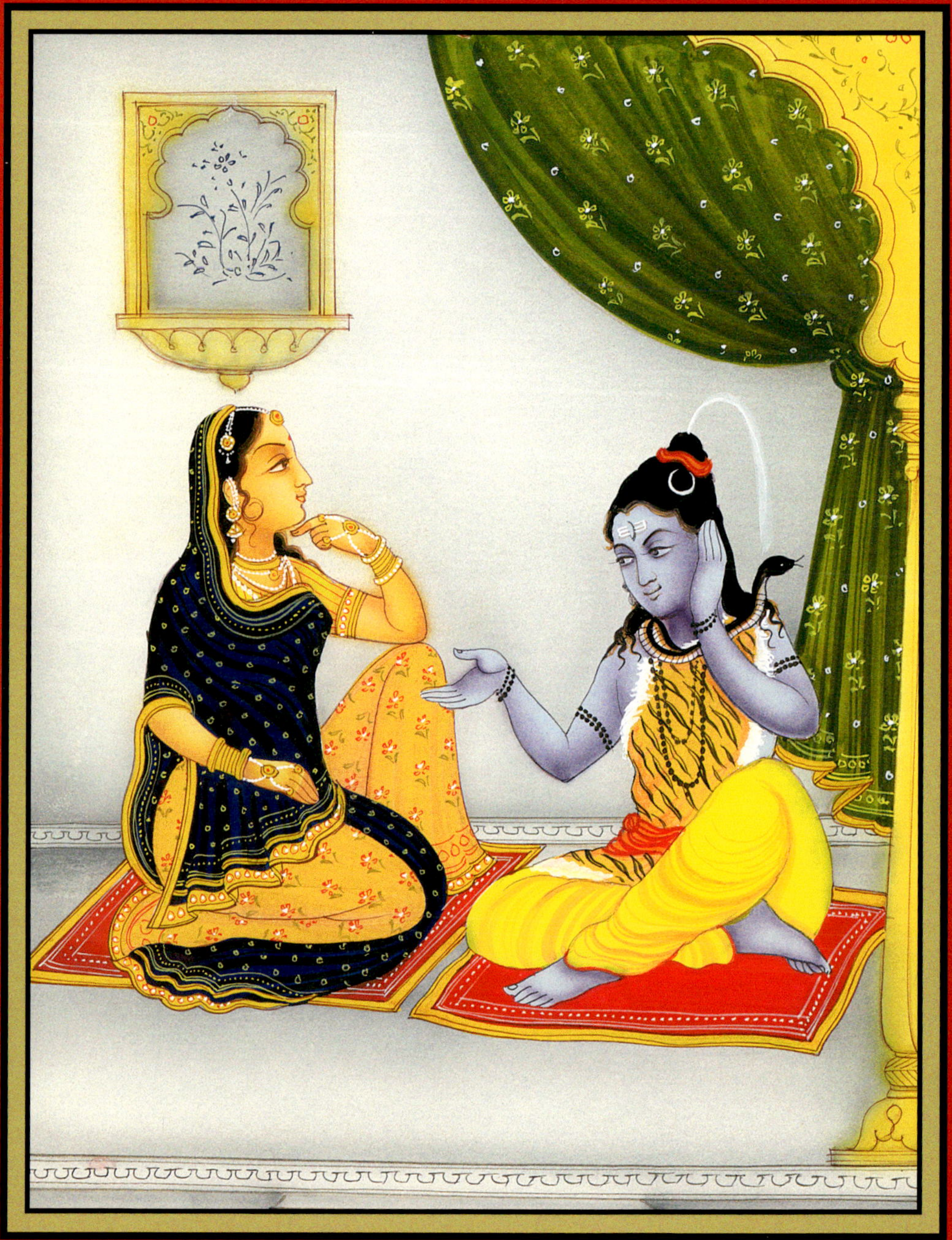

तू मेरा गीत है, गज़ल है, संगीत है।
तू ही तो मेरे मन मन्दिर का मीत है।।

प्रति
Pati
Husband

You are my song, my gazal, my music.
You are the part of the temple of my heart.

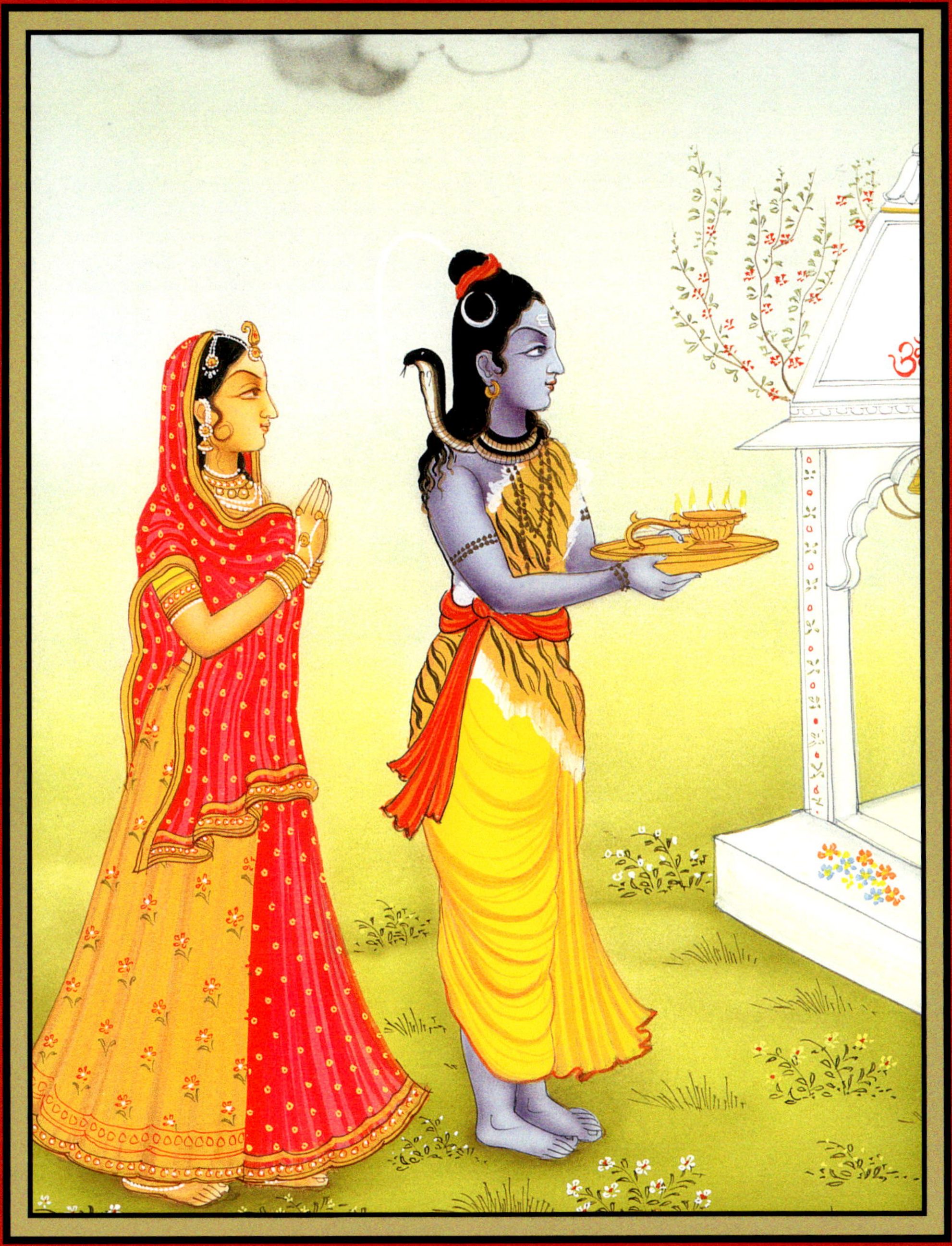

तू मेरी आरती है, प्रार्थना है, पूजा है।
तुझ बिन नहीं मेरा प्यार कोई दूजा है।।

पति
Pati
Husband

You are my aarati, my prayer, my worship.
Except you no one is and can be my love.

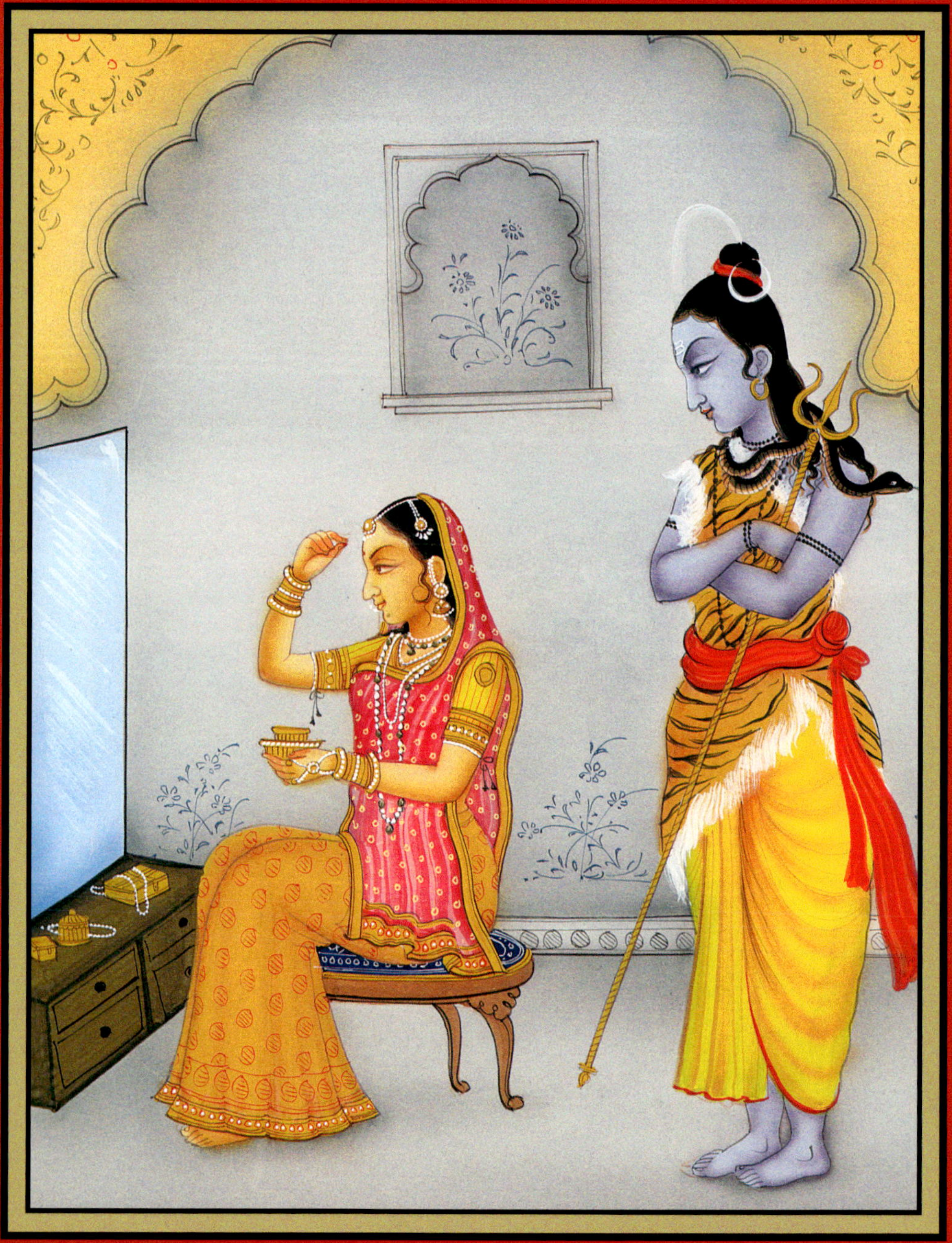

तू मेरा मान है, सम्मान है, अभिमान है।
तू है तो मेरी जान में जान है।।

Pati पति
Husband

You are my reputation, my honor, my pride.
My heart is beating only with your presence.

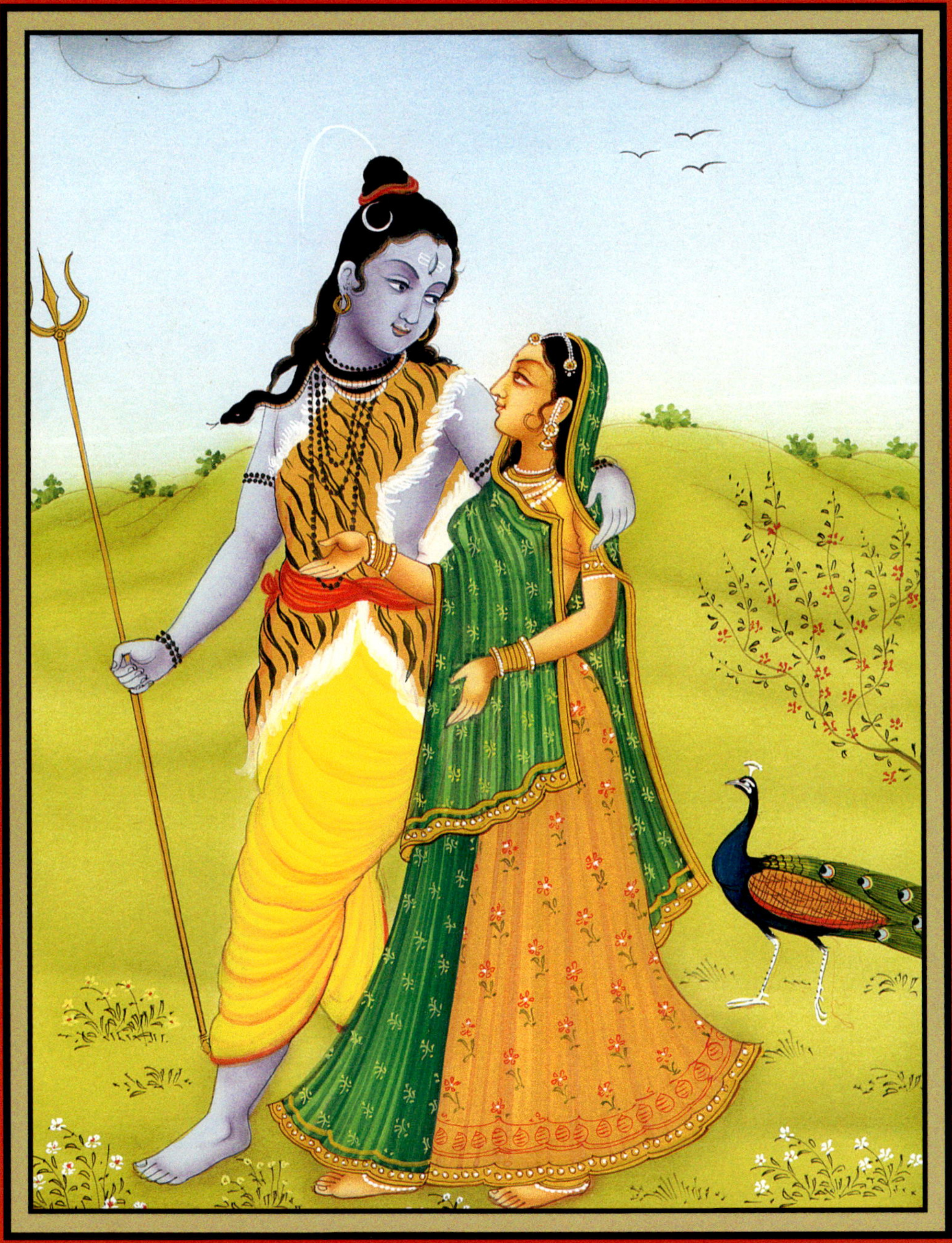

तू मेरा यार है, दोस्त है, मित्र है।
तुझसे ही मेरा जीवन रंगीन चलचित्र है।।

पति
Pati
Husband

You are my pal, my friend, my companion.
My life is converted to a colored movie with your association.

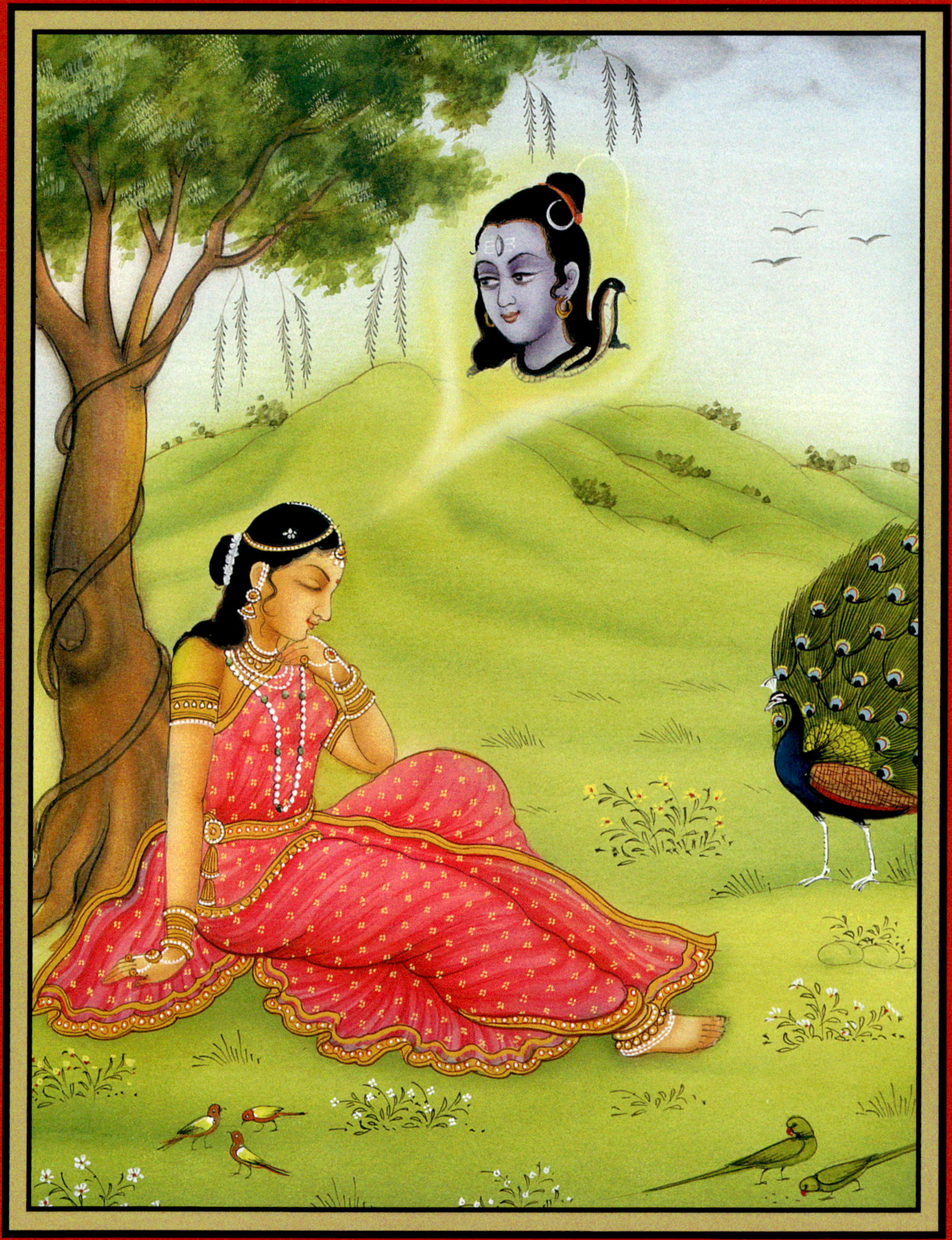

तू मेरी सोच है, अहसास है, चिंतन है।
तुझसे ही रहता खुशी से भरा मेरा मन है।।

Pati पति Husband

You are my dream, my feeling, my thought.
With you my heart always remains full of delight.

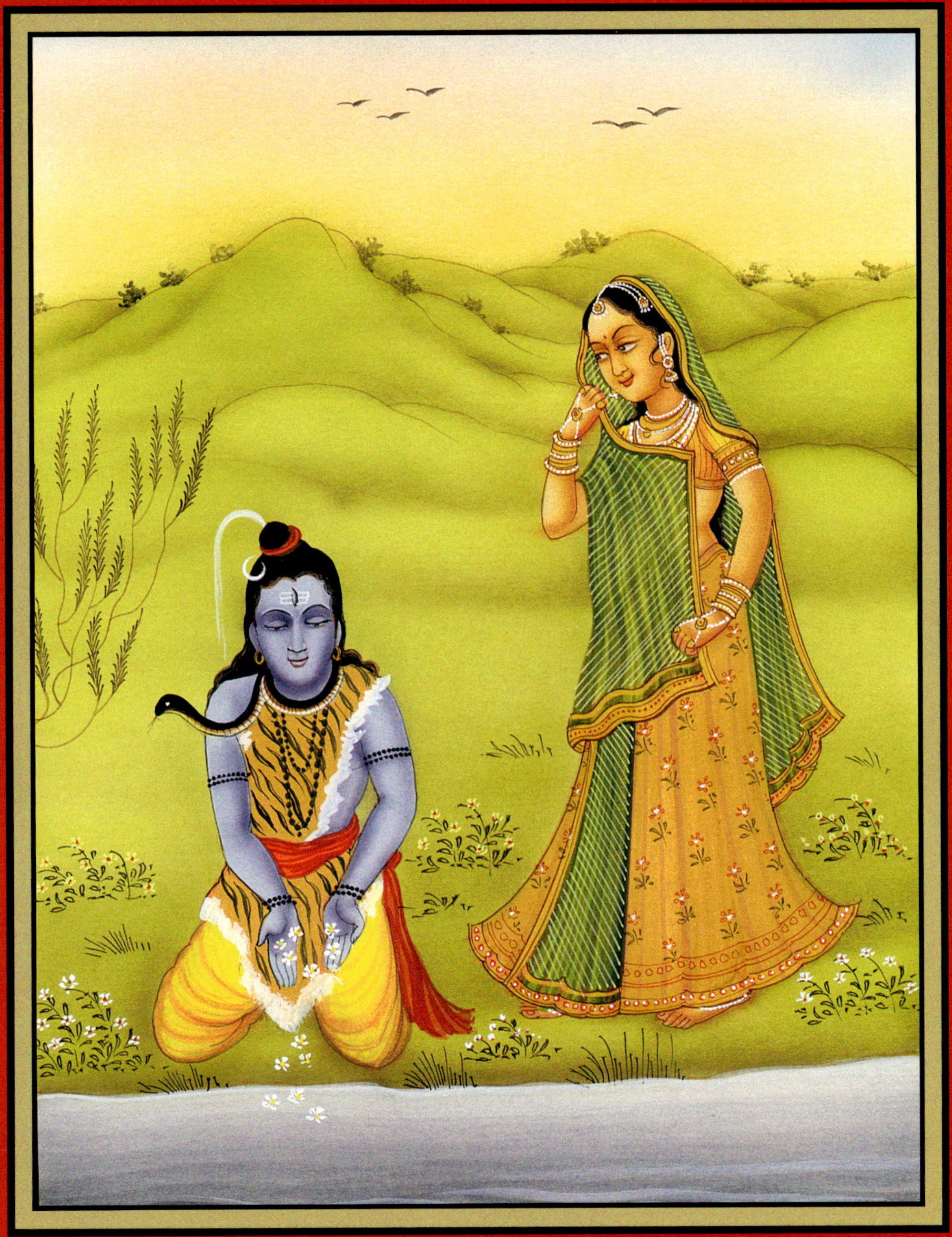

तू मेरी सेवा है, तपस्या है, समर्पण है।
मेरे जीवन की सारी खुशियां तुझे अर्पण है।।

पति
Pati
Husband

*You are my service, my penance, my devotion.
I offer and dedicate all my happiness to you.*

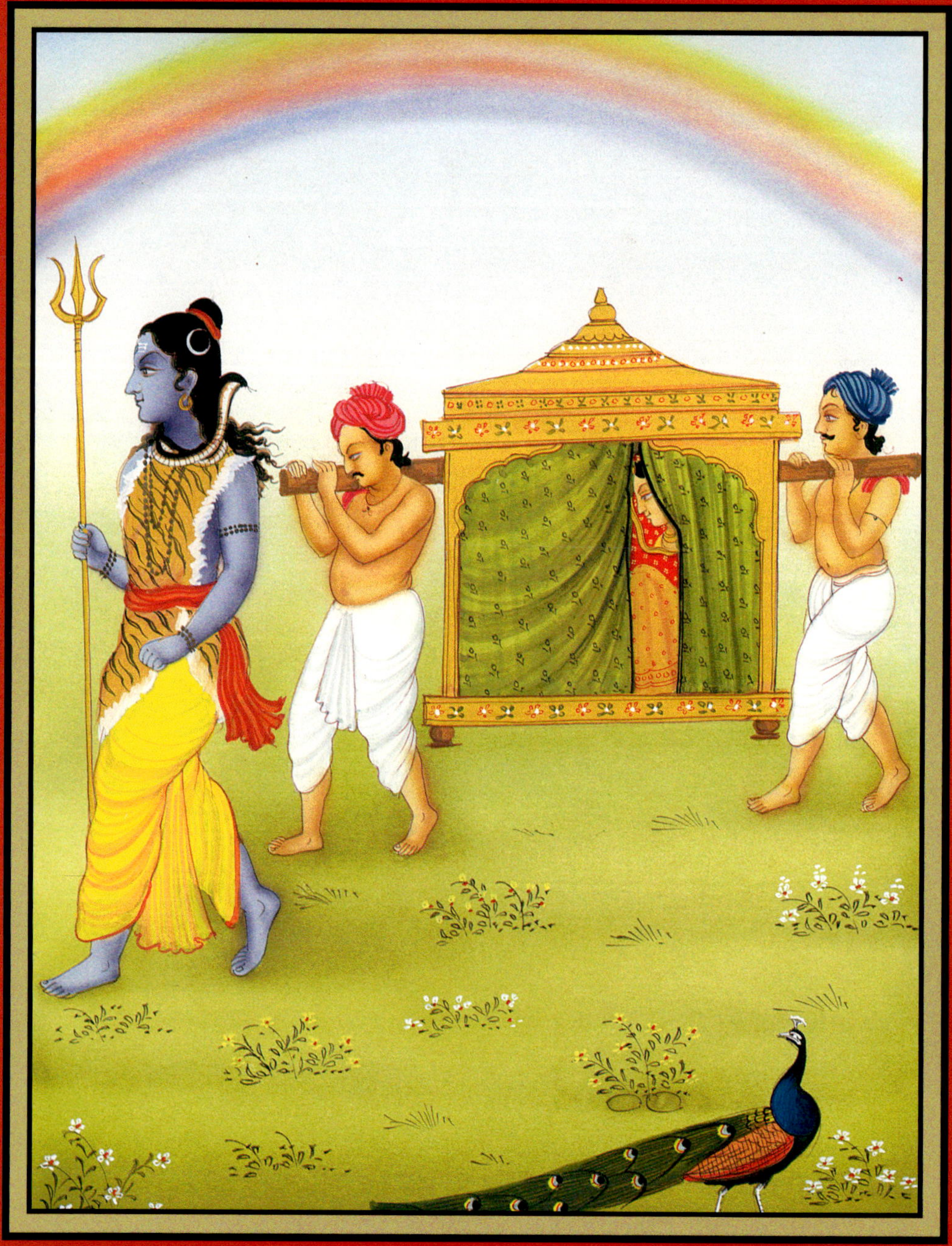

तू मेरा मौसम है, इन्द्रधनुष है, बहार है।
तेरा साथ ऐसा जैसे डोली संग कहार है।।

Pati प्रति Husband

You are my weather, my rainbow, my bloom.
You company is like palanquins with people carrying the same.

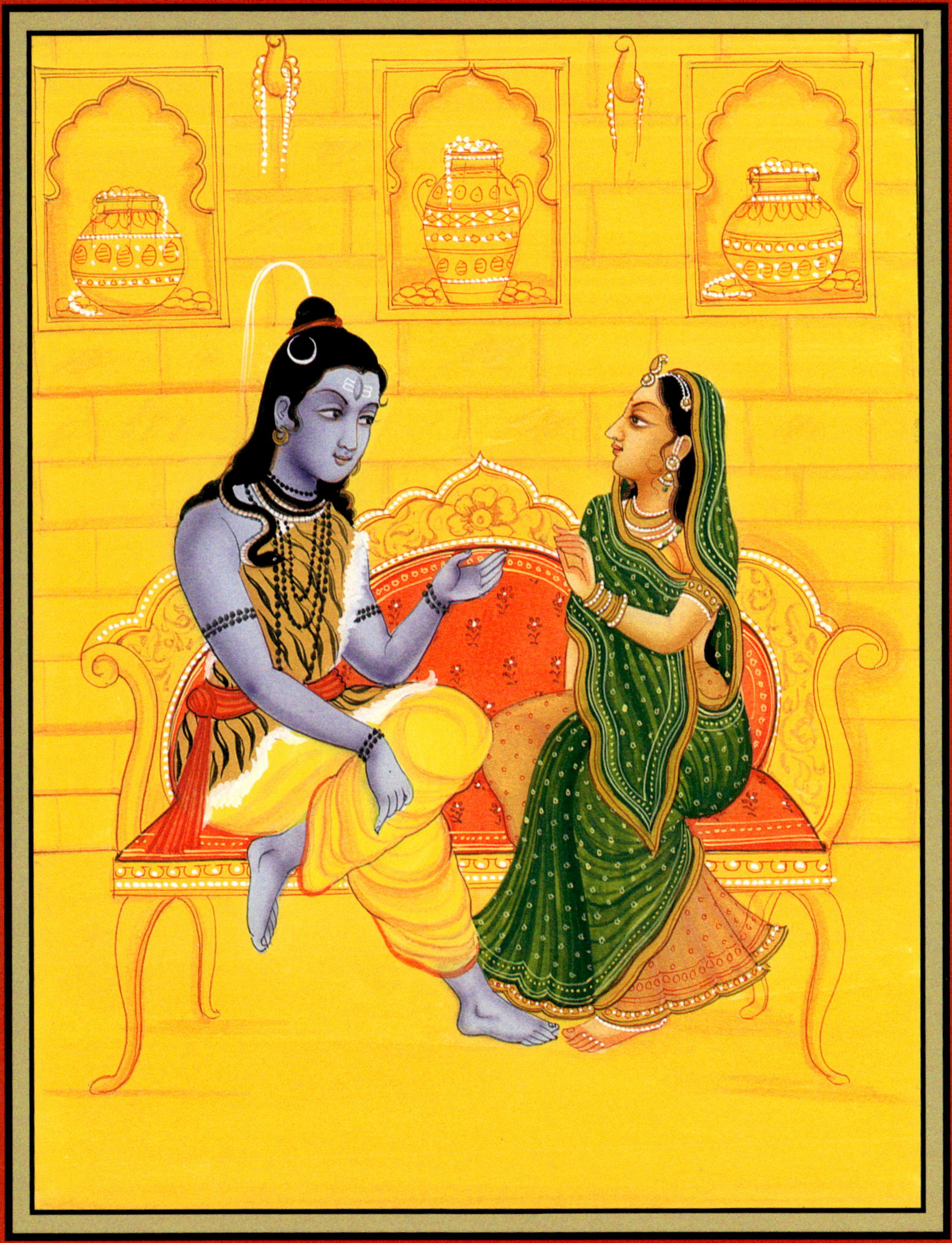

तू मेरा गर्व है, सर है, ईमान है।
तुझसे ही मेरे घर में सोने की खान है।।

Pati पति
Husband

You are my pride, my honesty, my head.
With you my house is a mine of gold.

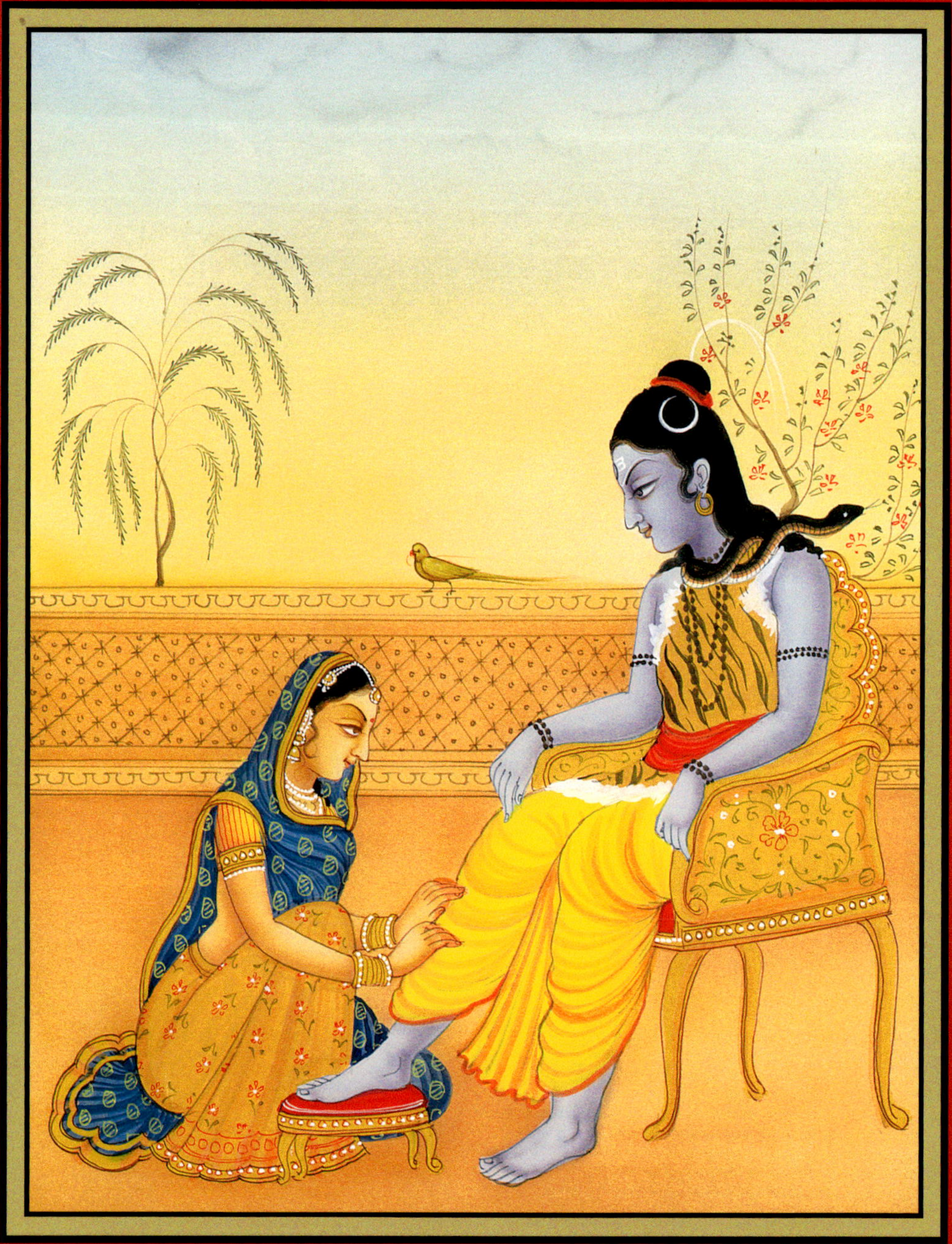

तू मेरा यश है, कीर्ति है, प्रसिद्धि है।
तेरे रहने से ही घर में नव निधि है।।

पति
Pati
Husband

You are my respect, my popularity, my fame.
Your presence ensures presence of nine gems.

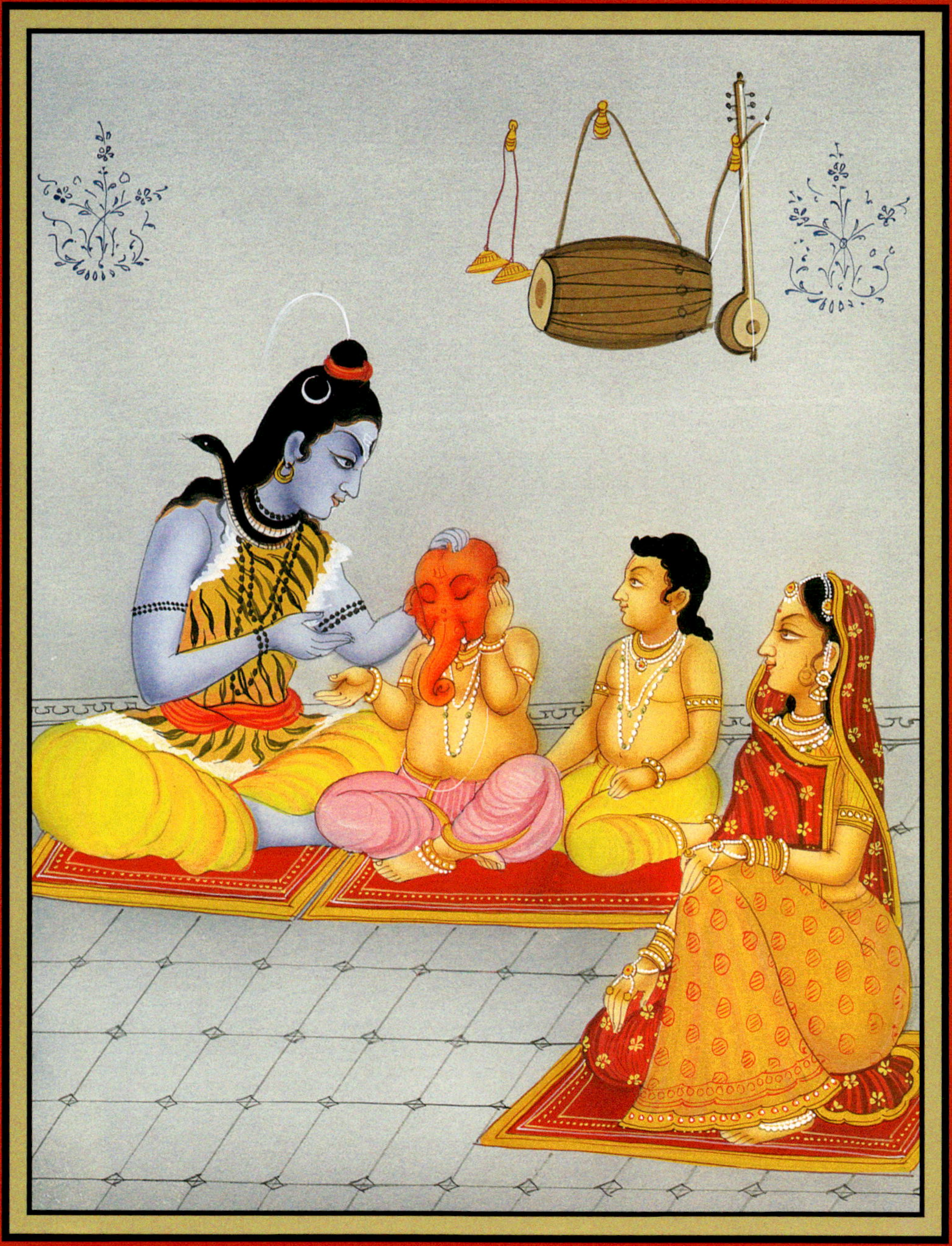

तू मेरा रास्ता है, प्रेरणा है, मंजिल है।
तुझसे ही घर में खुशियों की महफिल है।।

Pati पति Husband

You are my way, my speed, my destination.
With you the house is pavilion of dancing, singing and exhilaration.

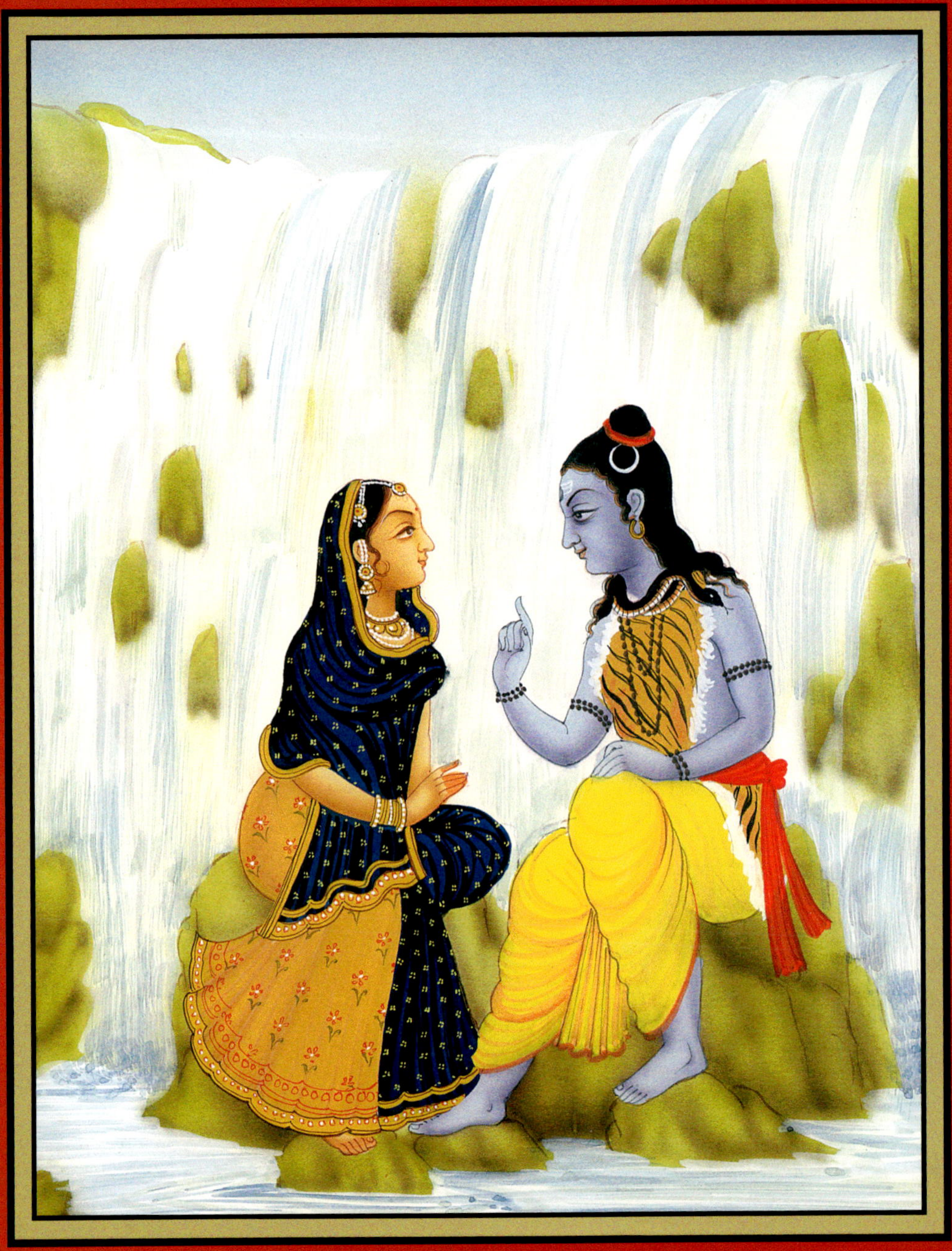

तू मेरी खुशी है, सृजन है, प्रेरणा है।
तू है तो बरसात बिन भी चलता ये झरना है।।

पति
Pati
Husband

You are my happiness, my creativity, my inspiration.
Your presence keeps the water fall flowing even without rain.

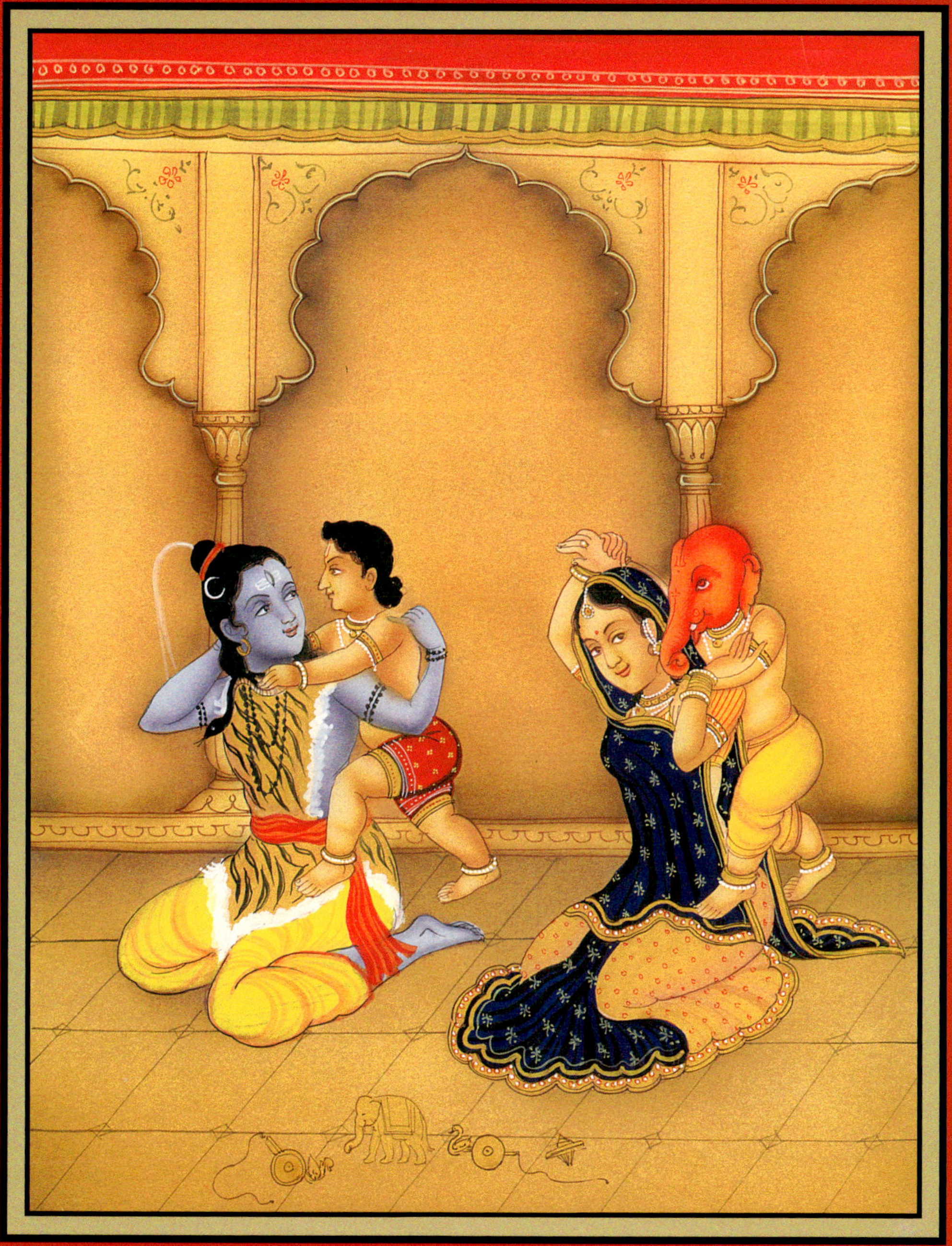

तू मेरा घर है, बच्चे हैं, परिवार है।
तेरा संग होने से ही जिंदगी का सार है।।

Pati पति
Husband

You are my home, my children, my family.
There is spirit in the life if lived with you jointly.

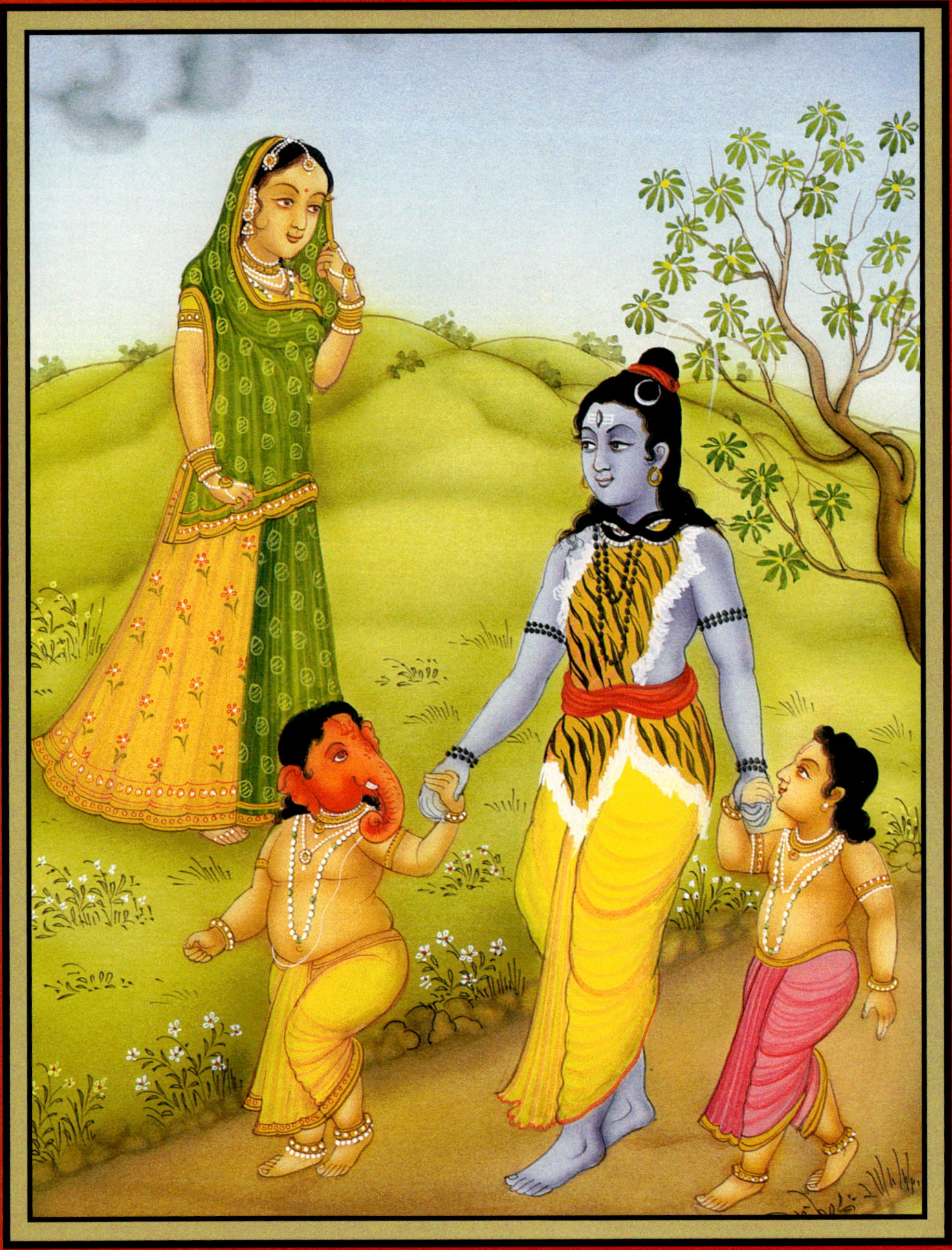

तू मेरा चरित्र है, पवित्रता है, संस्कार है।
तेरे होने से ही मेरा घर संसार है।।

पति
Pati
Husband

You are my character, my purity, my embellishment.
With you only is my home and the world.

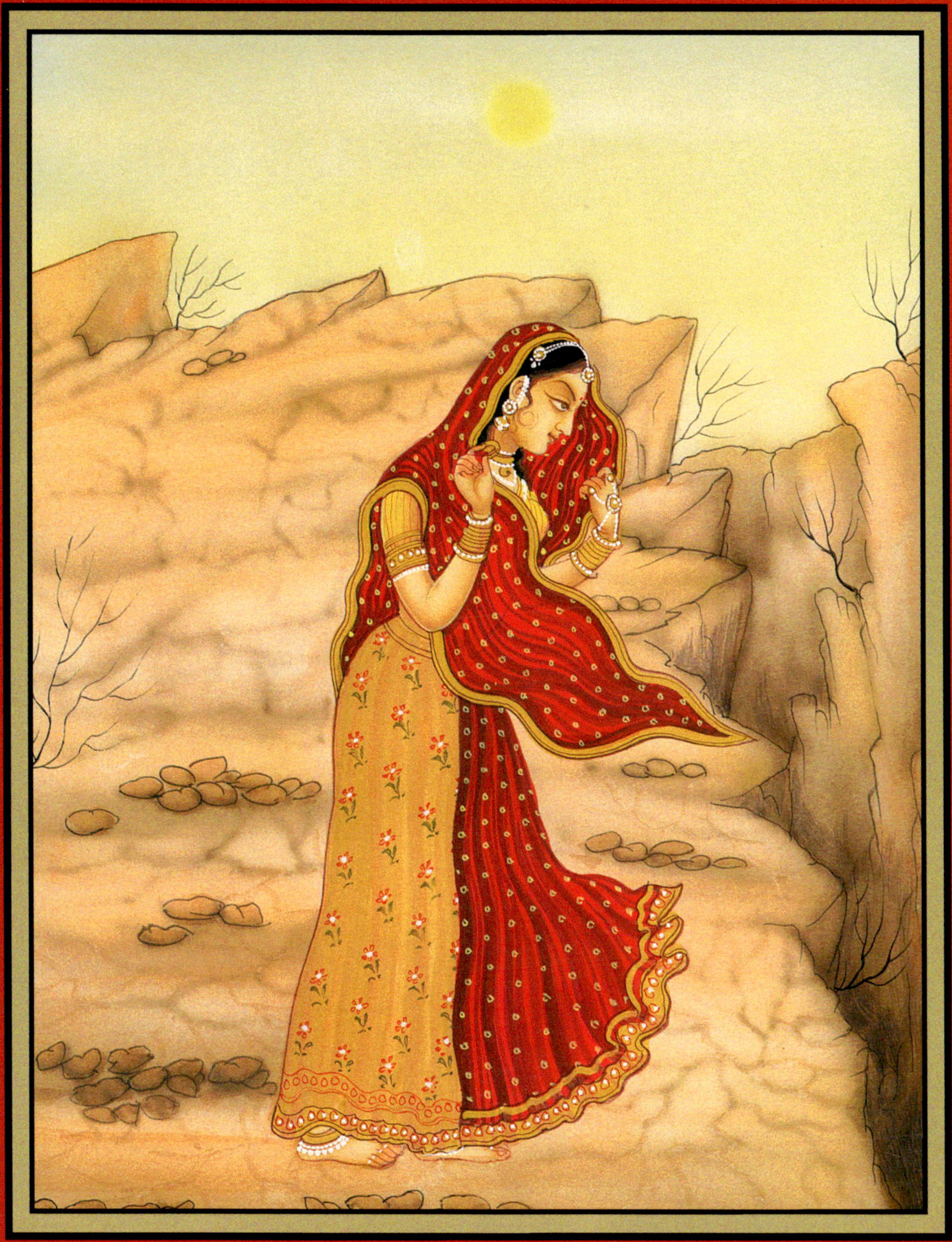

तू मेरा वादा है, व्यवहार है, सच्चाई है।
तुझ बिन ये जीवन दुखों की खाई है।।

Pati पति
Husband

You are my promise, my behavior, my truth.
The life is trench of sorrows without your path.

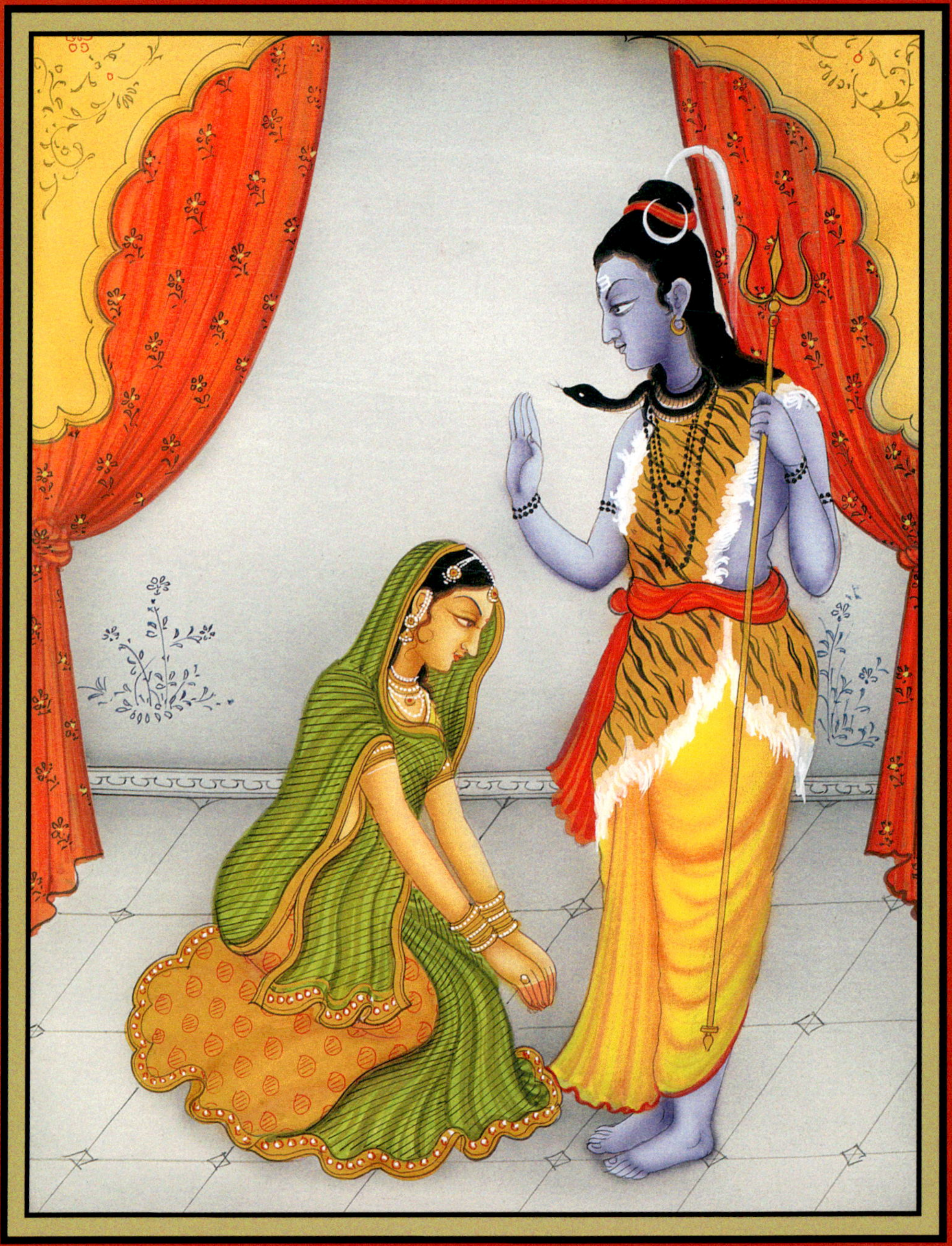

तू मेरी सोच है, आचार है, विचार है।
तेरे बिना जिंदगी में सब बेकार है।।

Pati पति Husband

You are my thinking, my action, my opinion.
Every thing in life is waste without you join.

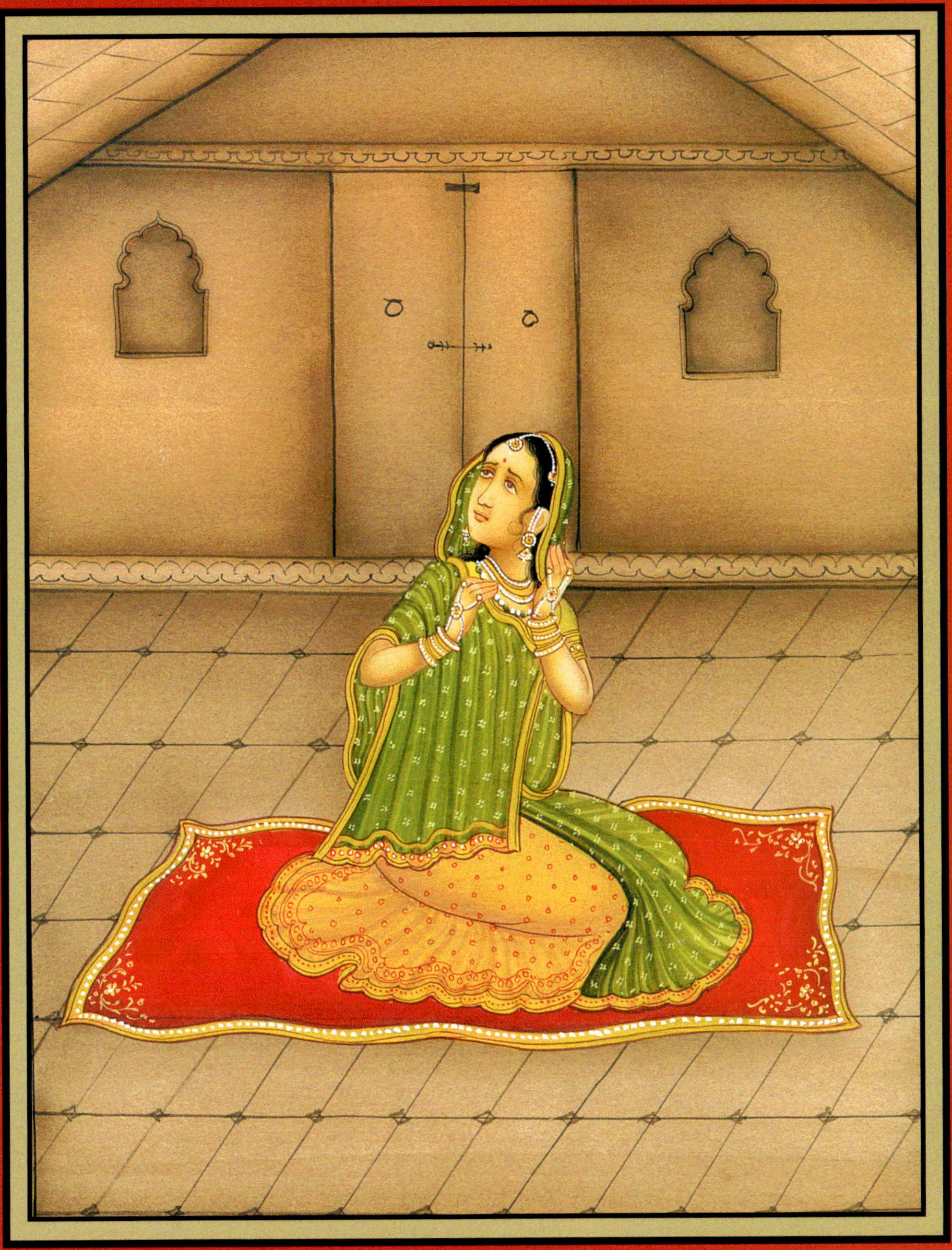

तू मेरा भाव है, भंगिमा है, भावना है।
तेरी अनुपस्थिति का सोच भी डरावना है।।

Pati पति Husband

You are my meaning, my emotion, my expression.
It is awful to even thinking about your absence.

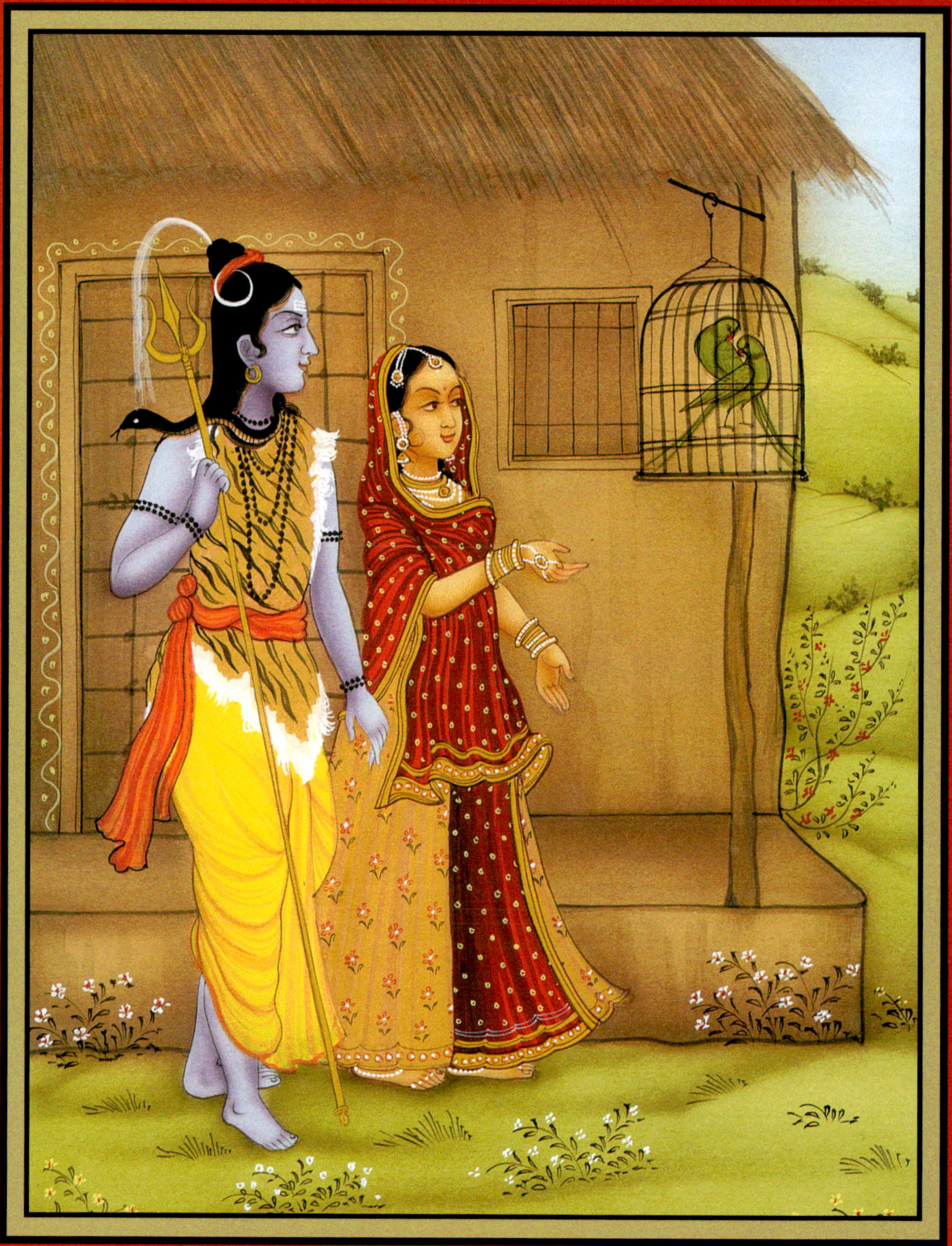

तू मेरा आनन्द है, खुशी है, हर्ष है।
तेरे संग जीवन में नहीं कोई संघर्ष है।।

पति
Pati
Husband

You are my pleasure, my happiness, my joy.
I need not struggle in life if together we enjoy.

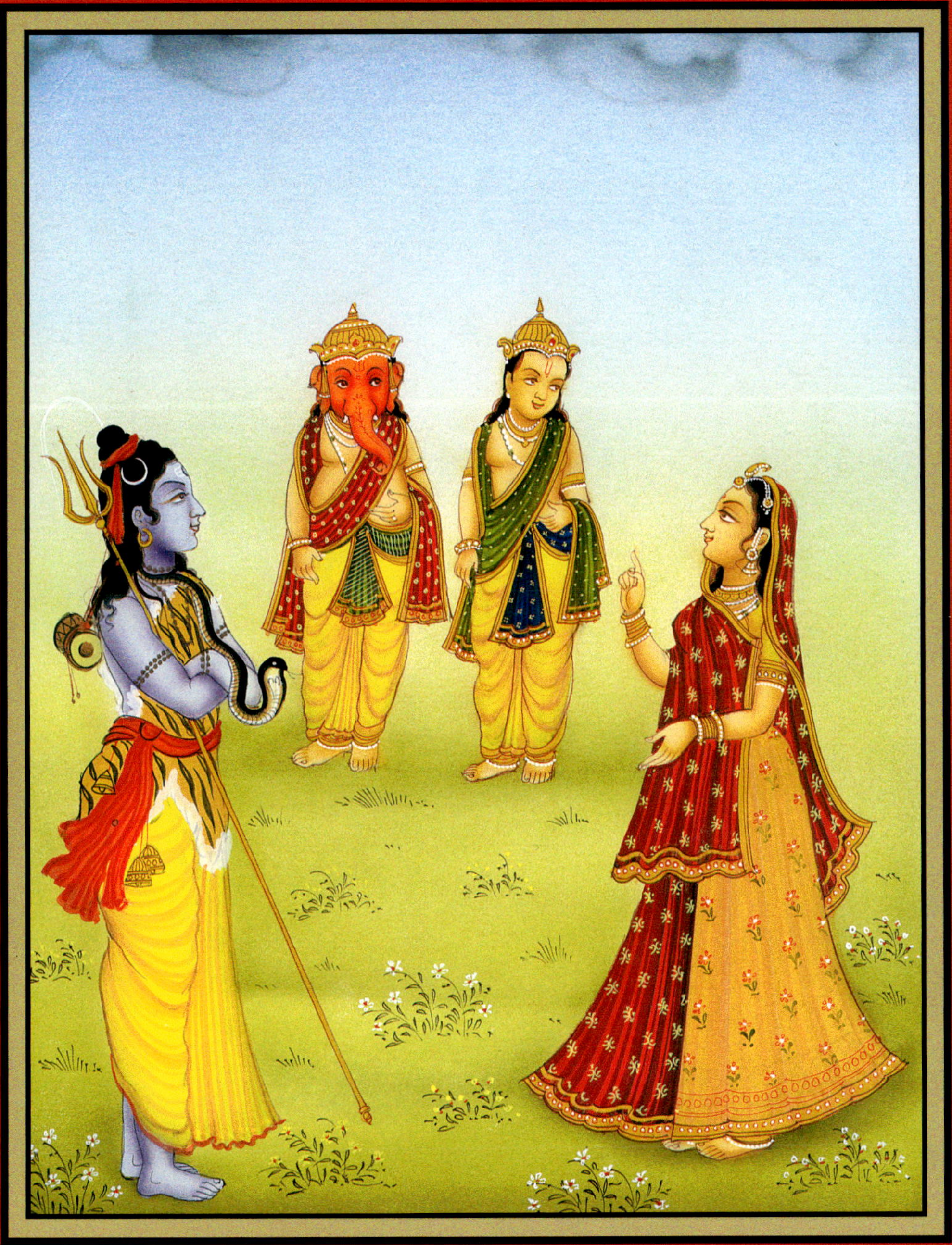

तू मेरा दिल है, दिमाग है, शरीर है।
तेरे साथ ही हम सब पूर्ण अमीर हैं।।

Pati पति
Husband

You are my heart, my mind, my body.
With you only, our family is truly rich and moneyed.

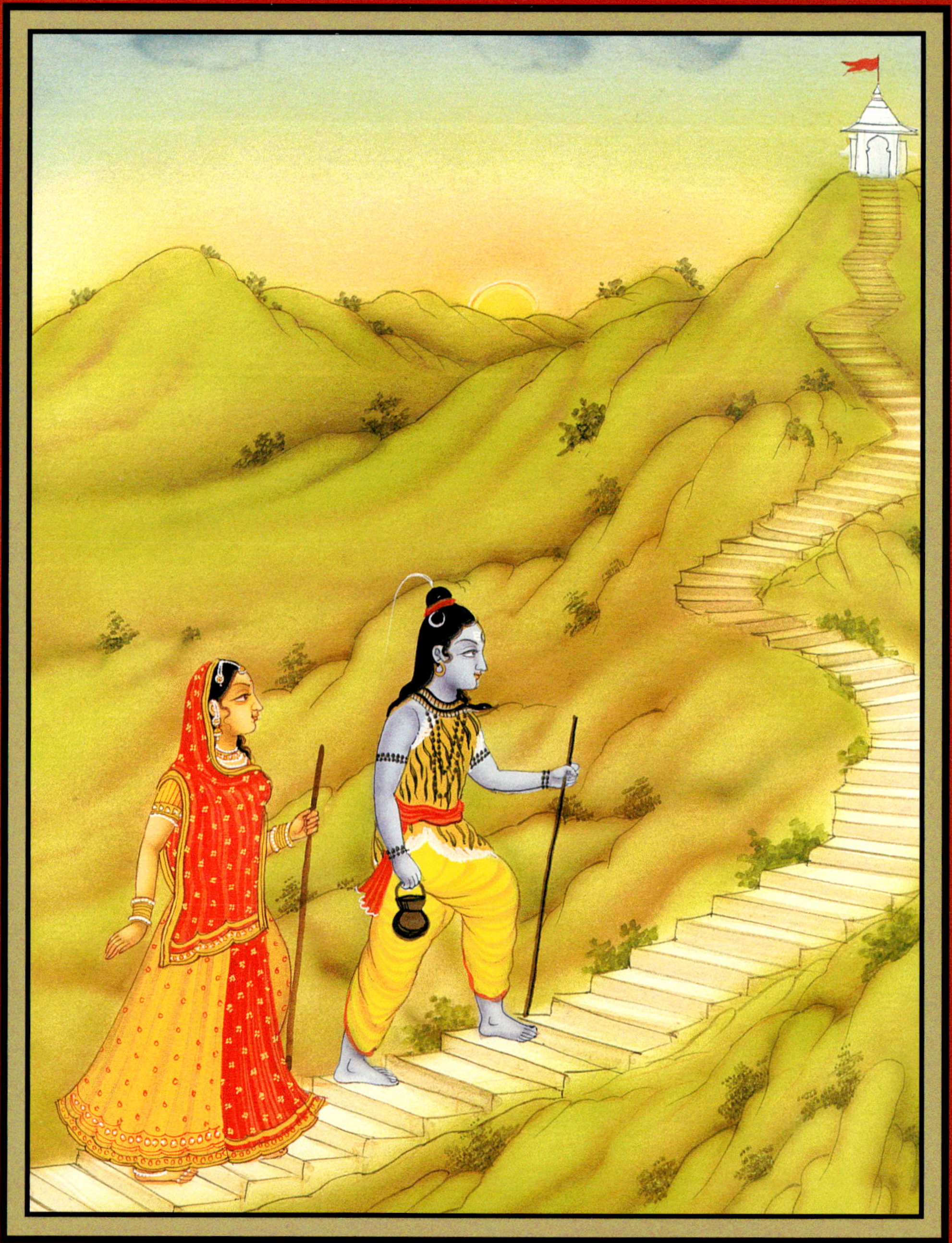

तू मेरा पुण्य है, तीर्थ है, धाम है।
तुझसे ही बनते मेरे जीवन के काम हैं।।

Pati पति Husband

You are my auspicious moment, my shrine, my holy place.
All actions in the life are successful with your best wishes.

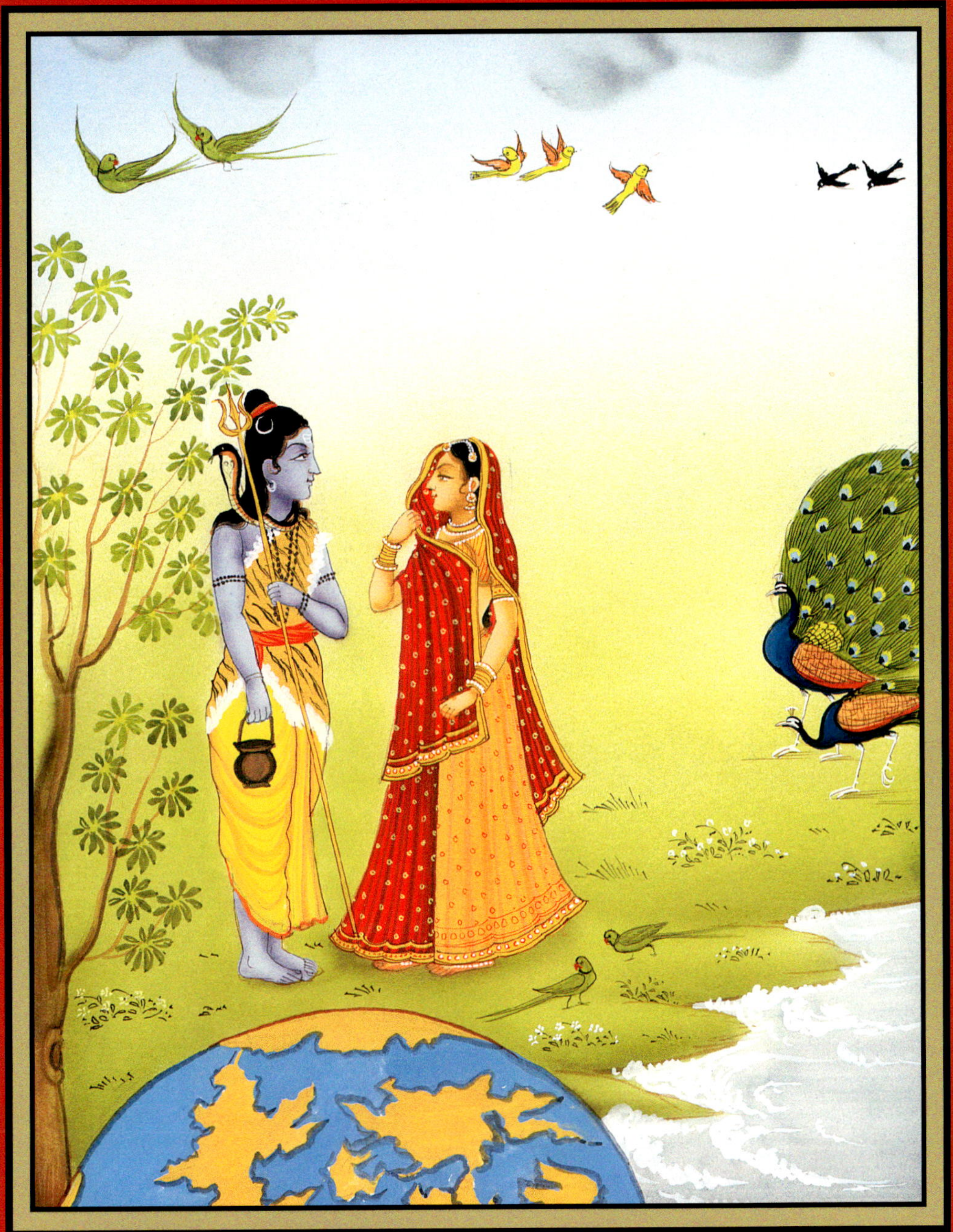

तू मेरा सूरज है, चांद है, तारा है।
तुझसे ही तो ये सारा विश्व हमारा है।

पति
Pati
Husband

You are my sun, my moon, my star.
The whole world looks & feels our own with your care.

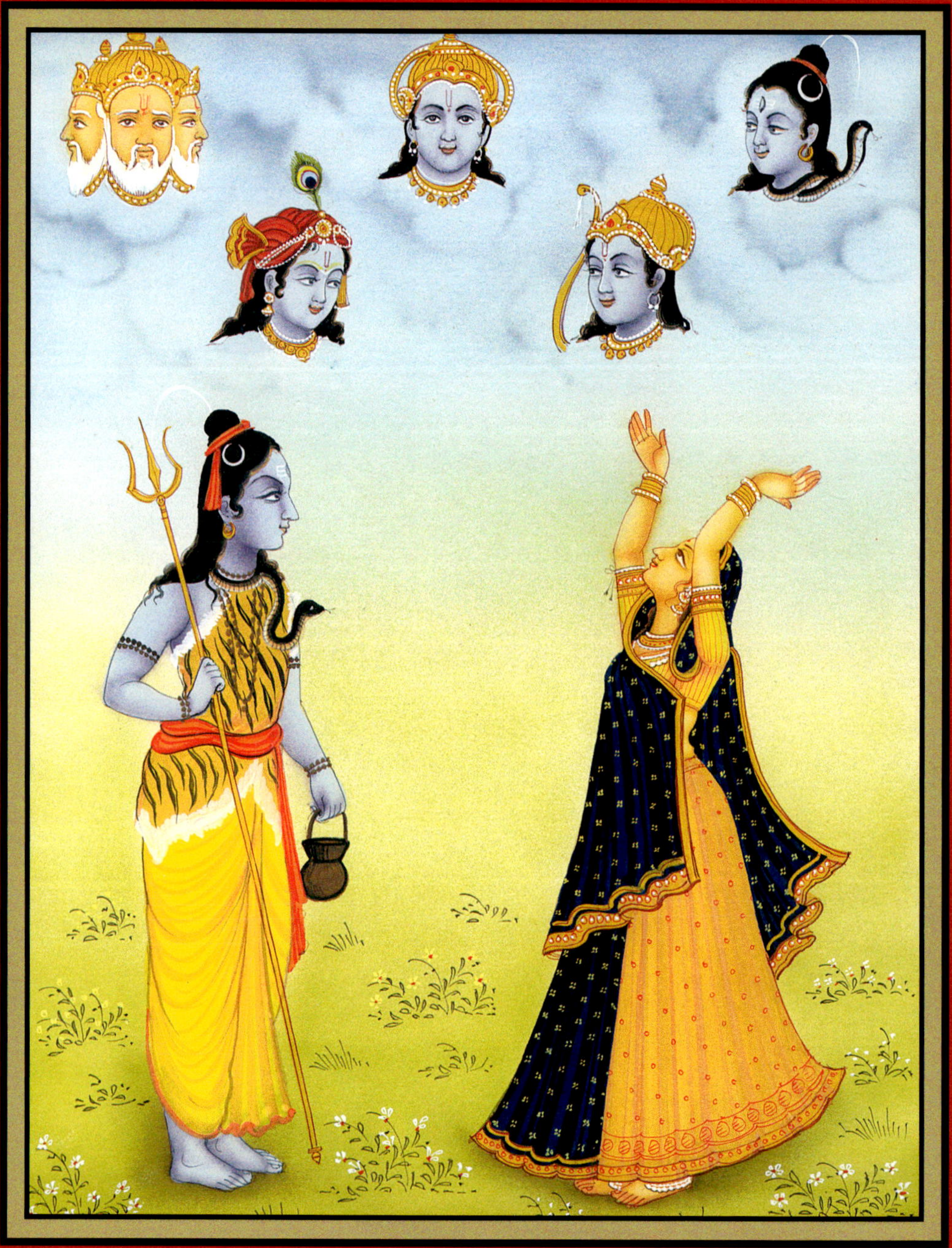

Pati पति Husband

तू मेरा यश है, आदर है, इज्जत है।
तू सदा मेरे साथ रहे, भगवान से यही मिन्नत है।।

You are my honor, my respect, my prestige.
You always live with me, this is my pray to the god.

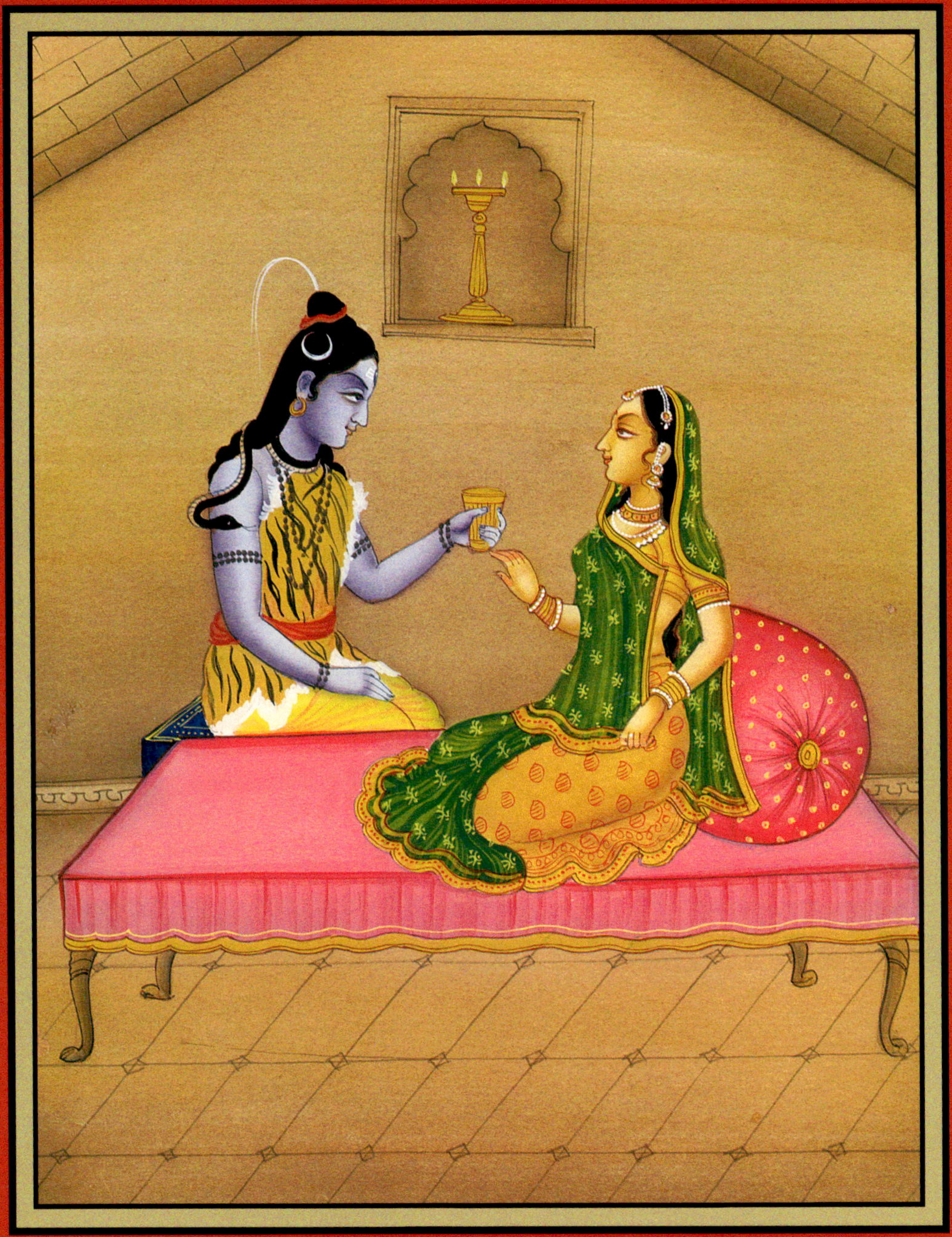

तू मेरी अग्नि है, जल है, हवा है।
तू ही मेरे सारे मर्ज़ों की दवा है।

पति
Pati
Husband

You are my fire, my water, my air.
You are the cure for all my maladies.

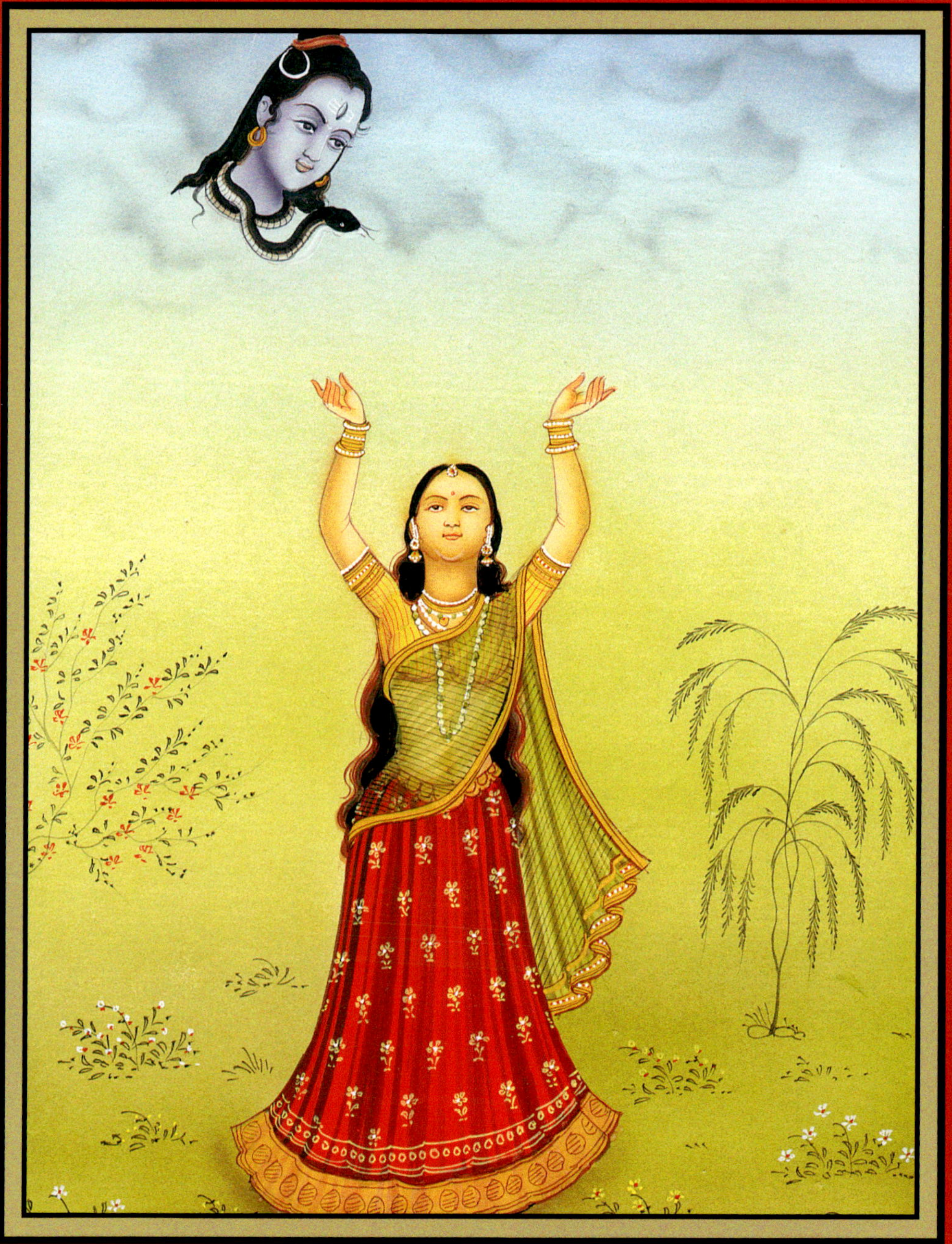

तू मेरा ब्रह्माण्ड है, पृथ्वी है, आकाश है।
तुझे कुछ हो जाये तो ये मेरा विनाश है।।

पति Pati Husband

You are my universe, my earth, my ether.
It is my destruction if any thing happens to you.

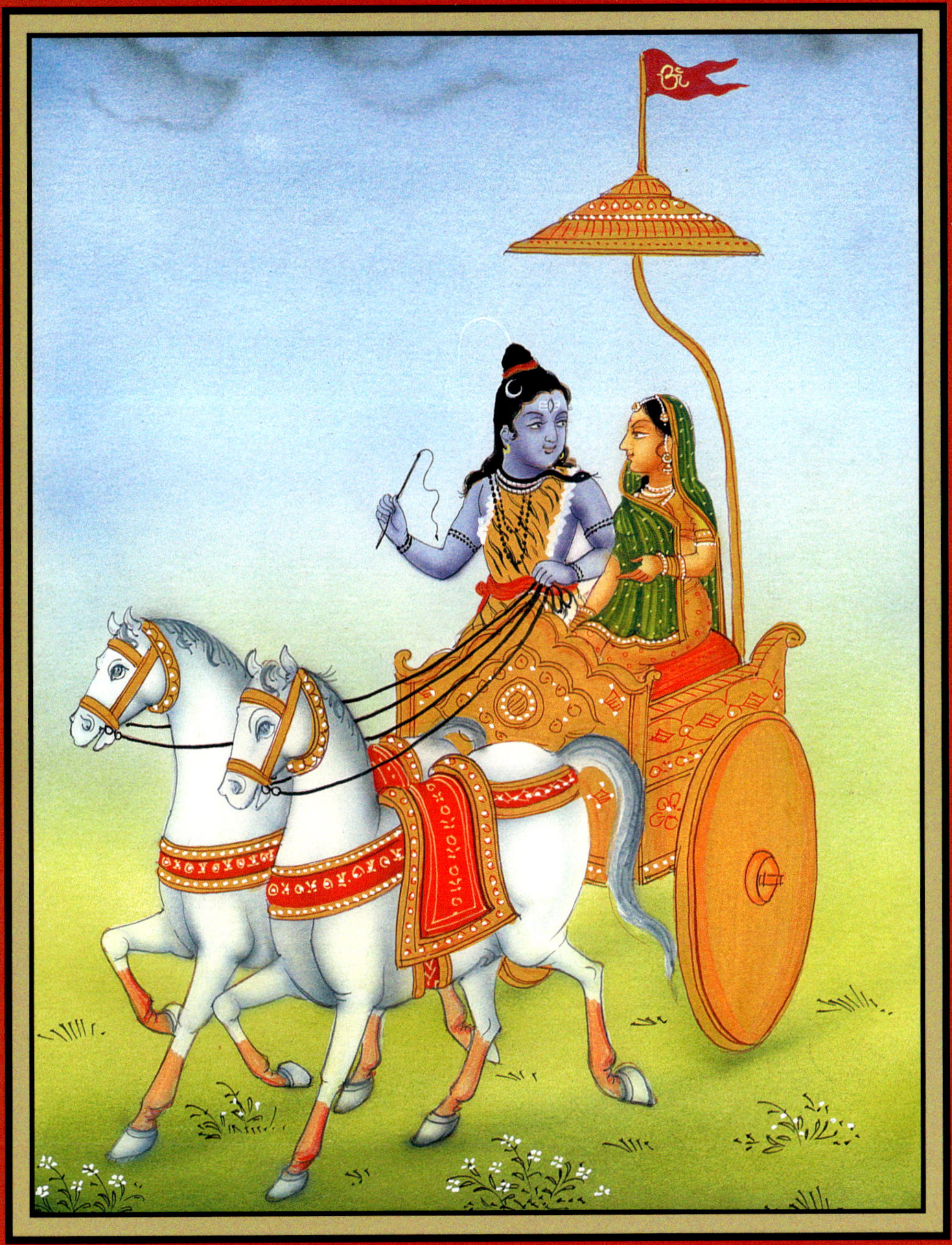

तू मेरी हँसी है, मुस्कान है, ठहाका है।
तू ही मेरी विजय की पताका है।।

पति
Pati
Husband

You are my laughter, my smile, my cachinnation.
You are the pennant of victory of journey of my life.

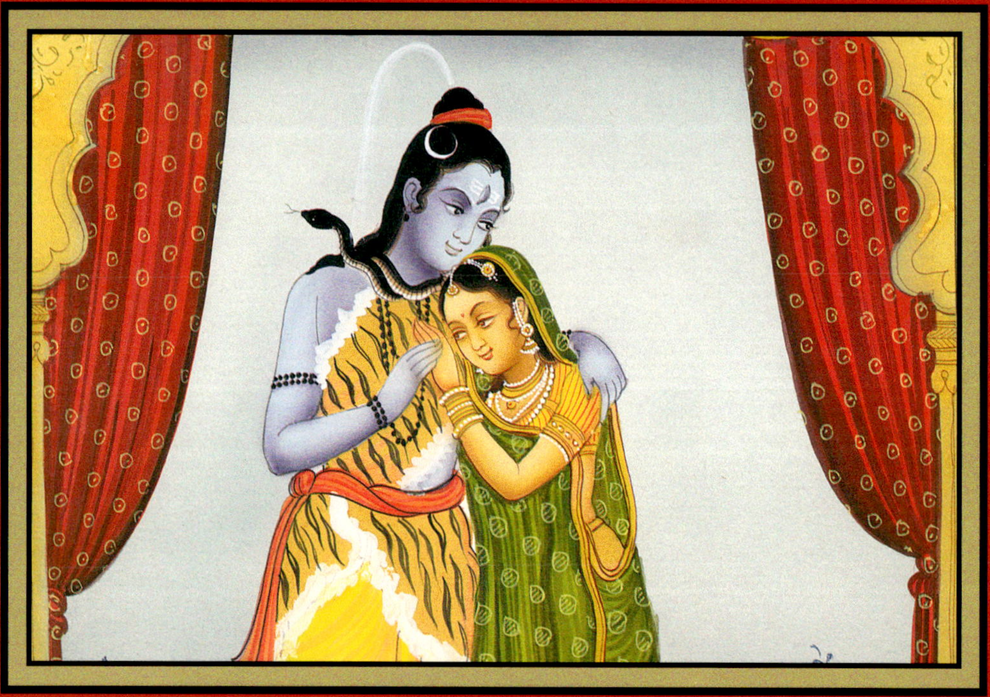

तेरे बिना कभी जीना न पड़े, यही मेरी दुआ है।
इतना ही नहीं
तेरे बिना जीने की मैं सोच नहीं सकती।
तेरे बिन जीना तो दूर, मैं आँखें खोल नहीं सकती।।
इसलिये दिल कभी तू तोड़ना न मेरा।
और मुझसे कभी मुंह न मोड़ना तेरा।।
भगवान से भी मैं यही प्रार्थना करती हूँ कि,
वो तेरे सारे गम दे दे मुझे।
और उसे अगर जरूरत है किसी की,
तो तुझसे पहले ही ले ले मुझे।।

I pray I am not forced by the conditions to live without you.
Not only living without you,
I should not be made to even open my eyes without you.
So, please do not break my heart any day
and
do not ignore me any way.
I only pray to god that he gives all your pains to me
and
If He needs someone, He should take me away before you.